THE

EVOLUTION

OF

APPLE iOS

VERSION 1 to 13

MICHAEL

JOSH

Copyright

Printed in the United States of America
© 2019 by Charles Smith

Churchgate Publishing House

USA | UK | Canada

i

Table of Contents

Why This Book?

Isn't it lovely enough if you are a fan of a brand and are proud to know about the birth of some specific facts of the brand? This book has made a workaround on the evolution of the Apple iPhone operating system. This book will infer the delivery of the iOS version you do receive on your device for a new update, which gives the system UI of your device a new look and system upgrade.

This book also gives an insight into when each version of the OS was released, when each model of the device stop support for each version.

About the Author

Michael josh is a tech explorer with over 12 years of experience in the ICT sector. He developed himself with his advancement in the field of information communication technology, which facilitates his writing skills. His hobby is exploring new things and fixing problems in its most straightforward form has been his focus ever since. Michael obtained a Bachelor's and a Master's Degree in Computer Science and Information Communication Technology from New Jersey Institute of Technology Newark, NJ.

.

Chapter 1

The Apple iOS 1 – JUNE 2007

Apple iOS 1 was released in 2007 by Steve Jobs along with the iPhone. Back then, the apple's mobile operating system version was not known as iOS. The main stage where the well-detailed history of apple iOS begins. The operating share alike Unix core compares to the complete fledged system version of the OS. In a press conference, Steve Jobs referred to the operating system like OS X. Along the line, when Apple launched the iPhone Software Development Kit (SDK), the name was changed iPhone OS. The iPhone 1 was the first iPhone, which was an essential device then. It confined thoughts and ideas from the mobile industry and made them more pocket friendly such as the camera, phone, internet, iPod, which are packed into one device which fits in your pocket, and it can be used anywhere.

Features introduced

- Core iOS UI
- iTunes Sync
- Multitouch Gestures
- Multitouch Keyboard
- Maps
- Mobile Safari
- iTunes WIFI Music Store
- Visual Voicemail
- Web Clips on Home Screen

Chapter 2

The Apple iOS 2 – JULY 2008

In July 2008, the capabilities of the Apple mobile operating system increased with the release of iPhone OS 2. The iPhone OS 2 was quite a superior version of iPhone OS 1, which gave birth to an iOS development company that influenced many companies and businesses looking at how to build their iOS apps. It featured 3rd-party apps that are known as the location service (with the aid of the newly added GPS element on iPhone 3G) and the app store. The territory of smartphones changed with this new version, which brought a revolution to mobile computing. During this time, iPhone users with the original version stick to the apps made by apple as any other apps aside; this will not work for the phone. Their was changed in the dimension of things after the released of the iPhone OS SDK which opened up its new platform to the external developer globally. Numerous iTunes music customers changed into potential app customers with the new app store.

Features introduced

- App Store
- Google Street View
- Microsoft Exchange Support
- Native Third-party Apps
- Dropped Call Fixes
- Podcast Downloads
- Battery Life and Speed Fixes

- iTunes Genius Playlist
- MobileMe

Chapter 3

The Apple iOS 3 – JULY 2009

This version was released in June 2009. Steve Jobs had big development for iPhone users that year, including some features which will be listed below. Apple store was a huge success to the company also. This version gives support to 3rd-party apps such as push notifications and searches toolbar (spotlight), which allows users to search the phone. This version supports the iPad first generation, which was released in 2010.

When iPad OS 3.2 has a new pattern and interface for a larger screen, skeuomorphism was introduced. New apps were designed and introduced to include the larger screen that was present in apple.

Features introduced

- Control voice Over Bluetooth
- Find My iPhone
- Landscape Keyboard
- Remote Lock
- Download of ringtone
- Genius Features
- Bluetooth and USB Tethering
- Push Notifications
- Spotlight Search
- Voice Control
- MMS, Paste, Cut, Copy

Chapter 4

The Apple iOS 4 – JUNE 2010

This version is the number four major release of the Apple iOS mobile operating system by the company. One of the most amazing things about the announcement of this version in June 2010 was that the need for iOS app creators was felt. Apple extended the compatibility of its operating system, which was a good idea as the software now compatible with iPods, iPads, and iPhones. In this version, apple mobilized its focus, giving the power Multi-Tasking, Airprint, Personal Hotspot, iBook, Airplay, and FaceTime to iPhone users. All these are the eminent part of apple devices today but were introduced back then in 2010 with iOS 4. This version also featured the new high-resolution retina screens.

Features introduced

- Retina Display Screen
- Airplay for third party apps
- Personal hotspot (GSM)
- HDR photos
- iTunes ping
- TV rentals
- Game Center
- iTunes home sharing
- Unified email inbox
- FaceTime video chat
- Multi-tasking

Dropped support for

➢ 1st Gen. iPod touch
➢ Original iPhone

Chapter 5

The Apple iOS 5 – OCT 2011

During the announcement of this version iOS 5 in October 2011, apple iPhone operating system is getting more popular. In this version, Apple introduced cloud storage, which is called iCloud. It also featured the ability to activate the wireless connection and syncing with iTunes with the aid of WIFI. Replacing voice control with a virtual assistant known as Siri was the breakthrough element of iOS 5. These features triggered the popularity of the phone as it gives answers to users' questions over both web and OS at a beta stage in a natural language. The primary apple features were introduced in this version of iOS, which are iMessage and notification center.

Features introduced

- iCloud
- iMessage
- iTunes WIFI sync
- PC-free
- Notification center
- Siri

Dropped support for

- 1st Gen. iPad
- 2nd and 3rd Gen. iPad touch
- IPhone 3G

Chapter 6

The Apple iOS 6 – SEPT 2012

iOS 6 was announced at Apple's developer conference in 2012. Series of changes were implemented in this version along with an improved map. In this version, the Apple pathway with google map which has been using since the beginning of 2007. 3D flyover mode, Siri's integration, and turn by turn navigations features were launched with iOS 6 along with the improved map service.

The beta version of Siri was introduced in iOS 5 but and upgraded version featured in iOS 6. The upgraded version supports users to get answers to their schedules and respond to command on your behalf and project a bright glimpse.

In this version, the apple passbook isn't left out though it was not that useful than in the mobile payment sector. The app supports payment types such as coupons, boarding passes, tickets, rewards cards, or QR code scanning. Apple also began to work on their closed source ecosystem by developing its notification widget for twitter and Facebook.

Features introduced

- Facetime over cellular
- Passbook
- Mail enhancements
- Homegrown maps
- iCloud tabs
- Turn by turn navigation

- Facebook and Twitter integration
- Upgraded Siri version

Dropped support for

➢ iPhone 4, iPhone 3GS and iPad 2 were limited to some features of iOS 6

Chapter 7

The Apple iOS 7 – SEPT 2013

Six years after the invention of Apple iOS, this version made an extreme change in the design with flat icons, simple design, and Helvetica fonts. Additionally, several new features and enhancement were added and brought around the existing apple feature set.

The control center featured a unique function that allows quick access to some apps such as; volume, brightness, Bluetooth, Do Not Disturb mode, and WIFI. The control center can be accessed with just a swipe up from the bottom. In this version, the Airdrop was also launched by Apple, which allows users to share files.

In addition to the little features above, this version put an end to the "update all" option in the apple store. So, apple enabled users to configure the update settings to either auto-update without being reminded to update a particular app.

One of the essential features the iOS 7 featured was the Touch ID, and it allows users to unlock their device using their thumbprint.

Features introduced

- Refresh core apps
- FaceTime Audio
- iTunes Radios
- AirDrop
- Control center
- Virtual overhaul

Dropped support for

➢ iPad 2 (limited to some features of iOS 7)

➢ iPhone 4

➢ iPhone 4s

➢ 3rd Gen. iPad

➢ iPhone 3Gs

Chapter 8

The Apple iOS 8 – SEPT 2014

The iOS 7 came with the massive improvement of the application platform to the visual changes. iOS 8 was released in 2014 with a redefined design, improvement in the workflows, and expanding the feature set. Apple developed this version to interacts with the iPad and Mac computers. Forget about Airdrop that allows the transfer of files wirelessly among users. It is now possible for users to cheaply pass information between mobile devices and desktops (computers). With this version of the operating system, users were able to take calls and send in messages from their Mac computers, unlike before it was limited to only mobile devices.

The supports for third-party widgets in the notification center was lifted, which offered weather updates, real-time information, and specific to stock information.

Furthermore, Apple launched the following features in iOS 8, such as; the Healthkit in the market and Homekit, together with family sharing functionalities.

The Siri that was launched in iOS 5 also had a major upgrade with the ability to purchase on iTunes over voice with Siri interface. All these make Siri what apple imagined in its virtual assistant.

Features introduced

- Family sharing
- Healthkit
- iCloud Drive
- Quicktype
- Homekit
- Extensibility
- Widgets
- Continuity

Dropped support for

➢ iPhone 4

Chapter 9

The Apple iOS 9 – SEPT 2015

This version of iOS was released in 2015. Apple works on the public demand on improving the technical foundation of the Apple operating system solid with comparison to the feature side of it all and working on the design.

With iOS 9, it came with the night shift, and the Notes app and Maps app was updated and passbook renamed to "wallet." This version solidifies the iOS future ahead. The lower power mode was launched to maintain quality performance even if the user in low battery. There was improved speed, stability, performance, and responsiveness.

In this version, the official public beta tester program was made available for users and developers who are interested in a testing run new updates and report bugs and fix it up before being roll out for the global update.

Additionally, Microsoft and Samsung had been offering multi-windows support for apps over the years, but with iOS 9 update, Apple made multi-windows available on iPhone.

Features introduced

- Public beta program
- Lower power mode
- Night shift

Dropped support for

➢ N/A

Chapter 10

The Apple iOS 10 – SEPT 2016

In September 2016, iOS 10 was launched, and by Tim Cook, it was considered as the OS with a major upgrade. This version improved the lock screen design interface and refreshed the look of music apps and news. The SDK (software development kit) was one of the major features of iOS 10 that was opened to developers in the first time with iMessage, Siri, and maps. Apple upgraded iMessage from a simple app, sticker with separate app store modified it into a full platform also open to third-party developers. iMessage was known as a competitive app with the likes of Facebook messenger, Snapchat.

During this period, Siri was one of the mobile virtual assistants but lost its stand as it was made unavailable for developers. It can also interact with non-Apple apps from the Apple store. Also, this time iOS 10 and Android N were compared between each other. Memories can now be accessible with the HomeKit enabled been managed by the home app.

The change in notification sees it displays videos and photos directly, and users had new ways to tweak their device by adding new effects, animation in messages known as emojis, and deleting built-in applications.

Features introduced

- Delete built-in Apps
- iMessage Apps

Dropped support for

- ➤ 1st Gen. iPad mini
- ➤ iPad 2
- ➤ 5th Gen. iPod touch
- ➤ iPhone 4s

Chapter 11

The Apple iOS 11 – SEPT 2017

iOS 11 was announced in 2017 at the WWDC. Quite so far, no one talks about 'files,' and this version was launched. This 'Files' is known as the go-to app, and it is used to search, organize, and browse files in their devices from the box application, iCloud Drive, and Dropbox. A new feature called 'Dock' was introduced in the iOS 11. Users were allowed to open and close applications instantly with just a swipe. This version also came with another feature, the drop and drag function. With this, users can move files, photos, and text from one application to another. Notes application also got aa major upgrade as users can now search handwriting and ability to mark and scan documents.

The ARkit was introduced, which was a primary addition in the iOS 11 version. This feature allows the developers to introduce the power of AR to a million users of iOS devices across the globe.

With iOS 11, apple pay was embedded in the messaging app, which made it easy for users to make payments or transfer to relatives or friends through messages. Apple pay cash card was introduced along, and it can be used to make payments or shop online. It also allows users to transfer money to their bank account. This version came with different enhancements such as Siri getting a new voice, redesign design for the app store, maps, and control center with the newer interface, settings. Besides, iOS 11 featured a series of new APIs like vision API, ML API, and identity lookup, and all these are influencing business in several numbers of different means.

During this time, Android and iOS 11 were compared, and iOS had the upper hand over Android.

Features introduced

- More enhancement on iPad
- Augmented reality
- Airplay two (2)

Dropped support for

- iPad 3
- iPad 4
- iPad 5
- iPad 5c

Chapter 12

The Apple iOS 12 – SEPT 2018

iOS 12 was announced on September 17, 2018. This version doesn't come with prominent features and improvement or revolutionary, unlike previous updates. Apple laid more emphasis on making an improvement and excellent performance to the often-used features. Wrinkles were also available for users to improve on how to use their devices.

Users were furious about AR compatible hardware for sharing experiences, image tracking functionalities and object detection were added to iOS 12 to make it more powerful. AR features were possible to experience with the aid of Pixar, which was lifted in to design a new file format for AR apps known as **usdz.**

The iPhone X users were blessed with the now-famous memoji characters as it was first introduced on the device. This memoji was the feature that influences iPhone victory when compared between iOS 12 and Android P. Also, FaceTime can open up to 32 users at once in a group through video or audio.

Apple also introduced Screen Time to monitor users Digital Health intact. It helps users to know how long they spend interacting with apps on their devices.

Features introduced

- Memoji
- Screen Time
- ARKit 2
- Group notifications
- Siri improvements

Dropped support for

- iPhone 5s
- iPhone 6 series
- 6th Gen. iPod touch
- iPad (due to iPad OS released)

Chapter 13

The Apple iOS 13 – SEPT 2019

iOS 13 was released on September 19, 2019. The Apple iPad no longer supports the Apple iPhone operating system, which is due to the released of iPad OS, which starts with version 13. This new iPad OS makes it a potential laptop replacement and a useful productivity device. It came many same features as iPhone OS 13 as it based on it. Though, it featured some iPad-specific settings. Also, the long-used iTunes store is no longer available.

Features introduced

- Sign in with Apple ser Account system
- New portrait lightning option
- New and improved Siri voice
- New security and privacy options
- Overhauled stocks Apps like Notes and remainder
- System-wide dark mode

Dropped support for

- iPhone 5s
- iPhone 6 series
- 6th Gen. iPad touch
- iPad (due to the released of iPad OS)

www.ingramcontent.com/pod-product-compliance
Lightning Source LLC
LaVergne TN
LVHW041221050326
832903LV00021B/731